German-American Genealogical Research
Monograph Number 6

EMIGRANTS FROM THE PRINCIPALITY OF HESSEN-HANAU, GERMANY, 1741–1767

Clifford Neal Smith

CLEARFIELD

EMIGRANTS FROM THE PRINCIPALITY OF
HESSEN-HANAU, GERMANY, 1741-1767

Clifford Neal Smith

Among the manuscripts in the Staatsarchiv Marburg, Germany,
is a large bound register[1] of the *Geheimer Rat* (Privy Council) of the
former principality of Hessen-Hanau containing information on immigrants to America (mainly Pennsylvania), Hungary, Lithuania, Pomerania,
and Russia, making it possible for genealogical researchers to deter-
mine places of origin and dates of emigration. Rubrik [section] XXXII,
Lit. A, of the Hanau manuscript is a chronological record of the decrees,
regulations, and administrative decisions of the Privy Council regarding
emigration matters. Rubrik XXXII, Lit. B, is a listing by name, place
of origin, and year of emigration. Lit. A is of lesser interest to the
genealogical researcher, excepting where decrees name the individuals
occasioning them, but Lit. B is of great importance; it is translated
hereinafter in its entirety, because the grouping together of the emigrants named therein often makes it possible conclusively to identify
them similarly juxtaposed in the ship lists in Strassburger's and
Hinke's *Pennsylvania German Pioneers*.[2] Researchers will want first to
consult the alphabetical listing of surnames which follows the verbatim
translation in order to discover names of interest. To this list has
been added notes on all those emigrants identified in the Strassburger
ship lists.

The Hanau manuscript has unexplained marginal numbers to many
entries. This might be a tally of the number of persons in the emi-
grating party, including women and children, accompanying the named
family heads. This suggestion is advanced, because comparison with
ship lists in *Pennsylvania German Pioneers* often discloses additional
males above the age of 16 years accompanying the heads of family,
whereas the Hanau manuscript, for the sake of brevity, does not include
these names. Marginal numbers in the original document are included
in the transcription within parentheses after the entries themselves.

+ + + + +

The *Grafschaft* (territory of a reigning count) of Hessen-Hanau was a much fragmented land. The main body of the country was about 65 kilometers (40 miles) long, running from the northern outskirts of the Imperial Free City of Frankfurt/Main to the eastern boundary of modern Hessen. At its widest point, extending directly northward from the city of Hanau, the principality was only 16 kilometers (10 miles) wide; its usual width for most of its length was no more than 4 to 6 kilometers (2-3 miles). In addition, there were several detached territories, the largest being 10 to 20 kilometers in eastern Hessen, plus about twelve much smaller exclaves, some no larger than a village and its fields.

The principality was ruled by sons of the Landgraves (Electors) of Hessen, but, since relations between fathers and sons were rarely amicable, the administration of Hessen-Hanau was quite separate from that of Kurhessen (Electoral Hessen or Hessen-Kassel). Economic and social conditions for the peasants of Hessen-Hanau were grinding; taxes and *Leibdienste* (personal services) were onerous; the soil was poor; religious conflict and non-conformity was rife, influenced no doubt by the asylum given to various sectarian *Inspirierten* (Inspired Ones) in the neighboring territories of the Princes von Isenburg (Ysenburg)-Büdingen-Meerholz-Wächtersbach.[3] As a consequence, some of the emigrants mentioned in the Hanau list which follows are likely to have been adherents of Mennonite, Dunkard, and other non-conforming splinter groups. The religious persuasions of the emigrants are, unfortunately, not mentioned in the official Privy Council record, however.[4]

Ironically, entries for immigrants to Hungary, Lithuania, Pomerania, and Russia may also be relevant to American genealogy, for it is likely that their descendants eventually found their ways to the United States and Canada during the nineteenth and twentieth centuries.

German and Swiss Mennonite groups which had immigrated to Russia in
the eighteenth century, for example, later emigrated to the American
and Canadian Great Plains in the 1870s, and the German-speaking popu-
lace (the so-called *Volksdeutsche*) in all the eastern European coun-
tries, uprooted during the second world war, brought thousands more
of the descendants of eighteenth-century Hessians, Palatines, and
Swabians to North America in the 1950s. Hessians in Pomerania, a
Prussian province now a part of Poland, would likely have immigrated
to America at any time during the nineteenth and twentieth centuries.

LIT. B: A PACKAGE UNDER THE HEADING
"SUBJECTS WHO HAVE FROM TIME TO TIME
APPLIED FOR EMIGRATION"[5]

		[Destina- tion]	[Year]
1.	Clemens Gieseman and Stephan Rüb of Rüdig- heim, as well as Joh[ann] Phil[ip] Bautz and Joh[ann] May of Hochstadt	Carolina	1741
2.	Twenty families from Ortenb[erg], Windecken, and Bergen district offices [*Ämtern*] to (6)	Hungary	1741
3.	Conrad Specht of Bergheim (6)	Hungary	1742
4.	Christian Matern, Jacob Scheppen, Joh[ann] Henr[ich] Wentzel, and Aug[ust] Bechtoldt from Orbenb[erg], to	Hungary	1742
5.	Henr[ich] Ohl from Kilianst[ädten] and Henr[ich] Kester from Wachenb[uchen?] to	Carolina	1742
6.	Ulrich Bar and Casp[ar] Lauch of Steinau (5)	Hungary	1744
7.	Joh[ann] Henr[ich] Schussler from Nieder- rodenb[ach]	Hungary	1744

8. Joh[ann] Wendel Heyer, Joh[ann] Phil[ip] Leiss, Thom[as] Schmidt, Joh[ann] Peter Hedderick, and Joh[ann] Georg Bender, all of Marcköbl [Marköbel] (See Lit. A, No. 5: "Several subjects from Marcköbl were given permission to emigrate to Hungary and it was simultaneously reordered that a table be prepared on such emigrants giving birth[date], age, [one word illegible] family, and assets, to be forwarded without delay." 1748 [no explanation of date discrepancy])	Hungary	1744
9. Balthasar Topfer of Rodenbach, as well as Joh[ann] Weber from Hochstadt and Maria Schaefferin from Rüdigheim [the word "Carolina" is pencilled in] (5)	Hungary Carolina?	1744
10. Mich[el] Haffner, Joh[ann] Guthmann, Ludw[ig] Schuhermann, and Christoph Hadermann, all from Schlücht[ern]	Hungary	1744
11. Peter Wirth, Paul Wegmann, Joh[ann] Dörr from Eydengesäss [Eidengesäss], as well as Joh[ann] Seiffart and Georg Iffland's widow from Altenhassel [Altenhasslau] (3)	Hungary	1745
12. Joh[ann] Martin Zeth from Seidenroth (5)	Hungary	1745
13. Lorentz Stock from Lützel (4)	Hungary	1745
14. Peter Koller from Lantzingen [Lanzingen] (4)	Hungary	1745
15. Jacob and Christian Euler, Nicolaus Haydt, and Joh[ann] Weber of Steinau (5)	Hungary	1745
16. Joh[ann] Valentin Steffel of Windecken	Pennsylvania	1746

17.	Joh[ann] Georg Völcker from the Büchelbach [area?] (4)	Hungary	1746
18.	Urban Euler from Marjoss to (5)	Hungary	1746
19.	Joh[ann] Phil[ip] Kalbhen from Gronau	Hungary	1746
20.	Joh[ann] Rüb, Joh[ann] Kollmann, Conrad Scheefer, Adam Hansel, Phil[ip] Heck, Christoph Ruth, Mich[el] Hansel, and Joh-[ann] Lotz from Rüdigheim, as well as Henr[ich] Schroeder from Rüngenheim. [This entry entirely marked out; a marginal note is illegible in the copy available to the translator.]	Pomerania	1747
21.	Joh[ann] Kunckel from Flörsbach, to (4)	Lithuania	1747
22.	Frantz Kückendörffer of Kesselstadt	Lithuania	1747
23.	Joh[ann] Casp[ar] Hartig? from Wagfelde? and Aug[ust] Emmerich from Bergheim	Pomerania	1747
24.	Mathaeus Knöpp of Kilianstädte[n]	Pennsylvania	1748
25.	Friedr[ich] Reitz, Georg Steigerwald, and Eberhard Kunckel from Flörsbach, as well as Peter Köhler from Kempfenbrunn. (4) [Note: Lit. A, No. 6 states "Several subjects from Flörsbach and Kempfen-brunn seek permission to emigrate to Pennsylvania and were thereby investi-gated as to who had encouraged them to do so. 1748"]	Pennsylvania	1748
26.	Friedr[ich] Bechtold of Bergen	Pennsylvania	1748
27.	Conrad Fischer of Litzelhausen [Lützel-hausen](3)	Hungary	1748

28. Conrad Jost from Windecken, as well as Adam
Förter, Peter Brodt and Joh[ann] Dörr from
Ostheim   Lithuania   1748

29. An[na] Cath[erina] Lentzin from Flörsbach
and Mechior Döll from Kassbach? [Rossbach?]
(4)   Pennsylvania   1748

30. Phil[ip] Wentzel, Mich[el] Urich, Lorentz
Wentzel and Nicolaus Christ from Rüdigheim   Pennsylvania   1748

31. Peter Strohl from Hochstadt and Thomas Cloos
from Bruchköbel   Pennsylvania   1748

32. Conrad Riess and Adam Kreckel of Lohrhaupten
(4)   Pennsylvania   1748

33. Joh[ann] Henr[ich] König and Jonas Dietz
from Hochstadt   Pennsylvania   1748

34. Aegidius Meffert of Wachenbuchen   Pennsylvania   1748

35. Sylvester Burghard of Windecken   Pennsylvania   1748

36. Friedr[ich] Höck of Holtzhausen (1)   Pennsylvania   1748

37. Joh[ann] Heyliger, Nicol[aus] Wetzel, Joh[ann]
Wilh[elm] Lotz and Joh[ann] Menge from Steinau,
as well as Joh[ann] Mart[in?] Henning from
Hohenzell and Joh[ann] Georg Frischkorn, Conrad
Hildebrand from Bellings (5)   Hungary   1749

38. Phil[ip] Lehning, Joh[ann] Henr[ich] Printz,
Joh[ann] Henr[ich] Eckel and Joh[ann] Mich[el]
Obernhäuser from Rossdorf?   Pennsylvania   1749

39. Theobald Schmitt of Kilianstädte[n] and Andreas
Meffert from Oberdorfelden   Pennsylvania   1749

40. Conrad Wiessner of Holtzhausen (1)   Pennsylvania   1749

41. Reinhard Rohrbach of Hochstadt and Velten Kaysser of Rüngenheim	Pennsylvania	1749
42. Joh[ann] Daniel Müller of Ortenberg (7)	Pennsylvania	1750
43. An[na] Margar[ete] Klingin from N[ie]dar- felde? [Niederdorfelden?]	Pennsylvania	1750
44. Strohlipps? widow of Rungenheim [entire entry crossed out. A note states "As in number 20"]	Pennsylvania	1750
45. Joh[ann] Bausum of Rodheim (1)	Pennsylvania	1750
46. Mich[el] Fischer of Kempfenbrunn and Hen- r[ich] Döll of Rossbach? (4)	Pennsylvania	1750
47. Peter Hartmann of Kempfenbrunn and Joh[ann] Huth of Flörsbach (4)	Pennsylvania	1750
48. George Kunckel from Flörsbach (4)	Pennsylvania	1750
49. Peter Beck, George [Engel] and Caspar Engel from Dörnigheim	Pennsylvania	1750
50. An[na] Elisab[eth] Lindin from [Bad] Selters (6)	Pennsylvania	1750
51. Joh[ann] Henr[ich] Deckmann from Blaichen- bach [Bleichenbach] (6)	Pennsylvania	1750
52. Joh[ann] Huffnagel, Hans George Frantz and Kollipse? widow from Neusses (3)	Hungary	1750
53. Joh[ann] Adam Köller from Lantzengesäss (4)	Pennsylvania	1750
54. Peter Herr of Kempfenbrunn	Pennsylvania	1750
55. Caspar Weymar from Lantzengesäss (4)	Pennsylvania	1751

56. Several subjects from district office [Amt]
Bieber [Note: See Lit. A., No. 7, which
reads: "Several subjects from Amt Bieber
seek to emigrate to Pennsylvania but, having property in excess of 500 florins are
to remain in the country [Hessen-Hanau];
thereby several reasons given why so many
subjects from this district office wish to
emigrate; no one to be given permission to
sell their possessions. 1751"](4)   Pennsylvania 1751

57. Mich[el] Anweiler and Anna Kleissin from
Eydengesäss [Eidengesäss] (3)   [Pennsylvania 1751]

58. Math[aeus] Bopp, Christoph Schum and Mich[el]
Stock of Breitenborn [Kreis Gelnhausen] (4)   Pennsylvania 1751

59. Phil[ip] Doll of Kempfenbrunn and Joh[ann]
Peter Kleinfeller of Flörsbach (4)   Pennsylvania 1751

60. Daniel Huth of Bieber (4)   Pennsylvania 1751

61. Jacob Bolaender of Eidengesäss [Note: Although the Lit. B list does not itself make
a cross reference, there is an entry at Lit.
A, No. 7-1/2 as follows: "Jacob Bollaender
from Eidengesäss was rendered a negative
resolution regarding his intended move; and
was denied permission to emigrate in view
of the directive to minimize emigration."](3)   Pennsylvania 1751

62. Christian Kautz, Wilh[elm] Lotz, Joh[ann]
Peter Cress? [or Kress], Joh[ann] Christoph
Riesling? [or Kiesling] Niclas Cress? [or
Kress] and Joh[ann] Huffnagel, all from
Steinau (5)   Pennsylvania 1752

[62a.   Among the resolutions in Lit. A is one (No. 3)
mentioning a person not otherwise given in the
Lit. B list of emigrants. The entry reads as
follows: "Regulation regarding those [persons]
who incite subjects [of Hessen-Hanau] to emigrate, occasioned by the case of the emissary
George Lubke, imprisoned at Kassel."]   --, 1753]

63.   Conrad Wehrheim, Conr[ad] Faulstroh, Joh[ann]
Justheimer, Conr[ad] Bruder, Phil[ip] Schraid,
and J? G. Waitzen [Waitz's] widow, all from
district office [Amt] Rodheim (1)   Pennsylvania, 1754-1755

64.   Conr[ad] Aumüller, Reinh[ard] Friedr[ich]
Fischer, Jacob Bolander, Joh[ann] Bock, J? G.
Gilzinger, Martin Ickus, Lorentz Arnold,
Conr[ad] Lohra, and Conr[ad] Haeuser, all from
the district office [Amt] Altenhasell [Alten-
hasslau]. [Note: There follows a barely leg-
ible notation, probably recording that they
had paid their 5th penny [20%] tax for emigration.] (3)   [Pennsylvania?] 1754

65.   Joh[ann] Henr[ich] Schaeffer of Rodheim and
Joh[ann] Henr[ich] Aschermann of Holtzhausen. [A note reads: "Regarding their
reentry permits."]   -- 1754

66.   Joh[ann] Seybold of [Bad] Vilbel   Pennsylvania 1754

67.   Joh[ann] Winckelmann's widow of Neuses (3)   Hungary 1761

68.   Joh[ann] Valentin Hora of Litzel [perhaps
Lützelhausen, Kreis Gelnhausen], as well as
Valentin [Bopp] and Niclas Bopp of Büchel-
bach (4)   Pennsylvania 1763

69. Phil[ip] Ohl, Andr[eas] Traut, Joh[ann] Phil[ip]
    Manckel, Conr[ad] Koppel and Joh[ann] Conr[ad]
    May, all from Kilianstädte[n]. [Lit A., No. 8,
    notes as follows: "Applications from several
    subjects of Kilianstädten for emigration to
    royal Prussian territory; bearing the recommenda-
    tion of the royal Prussian Resident von Born in
    Frankfurt, providing this is permitted by corres-
    pondence with the royal Prussian ministry and
    detailed remarks of his Royal Highness of Prussia
    and the Illustrious Landgrave [of Hessen] Wilhelm
    VIII regarding mutually permitted movements of
    their subjects according to the Convention of
    17 December 1755."]   Pomerania 1764

70. Erasmus Döll and Joh[ann] Heinr[ich] Lauffer
    from Bergheim [Note: "Regarding their reentry
    permits."]   -- 1764

71. Joh[ann] Phil[ip] Bender from Marcköbel [Note:
    "To be readmitted."]   -- 1764

72. Joh[ann] George Krafft, Joh[ann] Henr[ich]
    Emrich, Joh[ann] Velten, Joh[ann] George Hess,
    Joh[ann] George Neumann's widow and Joh[ann]
    Hess's widow, all from Blaichenbach [Bleichen-
    bach] (6)   Hungary 1765

73. Joh[ann] Henr[ich] Krafft of Blaichenbach
    [Bleichenbach]   Prussian Pomerania, 1765

74. Valentin Rehbock [Note: See Lit. A., No. 9,
    which reads as follows: "Regulation regard-
    ing the return of an emigrating subject,
    dated 18 Apr 176-, towit: Punishment of the
    former miner Valentin Rehbock of Bieber, who
    sought to cause others to emigrate."] (4)   Pennsylvania 1765

74-1/2. Joh[ann] Friedr[ich Ickus of Lantzingen
[Note reads as follows: "Stated reason
for his projected move to Pennsylvania
.and the investigation thereof, see Rubr[ic]
XXVIII, Lit. KKK."]   (4)   [Pennsylvania] 1765

75. Niclas Stock of Gassen [Giessen?] and Lentz's
widow of Ross[bach?]   (4)   Pennsylvania 1765

76. Several subjects [unnamed] from the regional
offices [Ämtern] of Ortenberg and Windecken.
[Note: See Lit. A, No. 10, not translated
here.]   Russia, 1766

77. Wendel Michler, Conrad Adolph [Schmidt?] and
Ludwig Schmidt of Inckheim?   Prussian Pomerania, 1766

78. Joh[ann] Horch, Wilh[elm] Brettmann, Wilh[elm]
Heyer, and Joh[ann] Henr[ich] Dietrich of
Marcköbel   Russia, 1766

79. Joh[ann] Henr[ich] Ulrich, Joh[ann] Flach,
and wives of Blaichenbach [Bleichenbach],
emigration applications of (6)   --, 1766

80. Joh[ann] Jacob Emrich and wife of Hecken-
bergheim, Amt Ortenberg, apply for a cer-
tificate . . . for their projected emigra-
tion to (6)   Russia, 1766

81. Application of the subjects Christoph Roth
and wife of Rüdigheim for permit to emigrate to   Russia, 1766

82. Application supported by prominent persons
of the community of Gelnhaar asking for
approval of emigration permits for certain
subjects [of that town] to (6)   Russia, 1766

83. Similar application from the mayor and council
    of Ortenberg (7)   [Russia?] 1766

84. Applications for emigration [submitted by]
    Peter Schwind and Joh[ann] Michler of Mittel-
    buchen   --, 1766

85. Valentin Hartmann from Elenstadt? seeks permit
    to emigrate (2)   --, 1766

86. Applications for emigration of the subjects
    Joh[ann] Bauer and Joh[ann] Steigerwald from
    Flörsbach (4)   --, 1766

87. Several subjects of Lohrhaupten and Flörsbach,
    namely (1) Joh[ann] Adam Dietrich, (2) Melchior
    Schuster's widow, (3) Joh[ann] Henss, and (4)
    Friedrich Steigerwald, together with their fam-
    ilies, including Joh[ann] Peter Schuster,
    presently with the battalion, are granted
    [permission] to emigrate to (4)   New England, 1766
                                               [in fact, Pennsylvania]

88. Records the secret [illegal] emigration of
    Joh[ann] Henr[ich] Staaf of Niederzell to   Russia, 1766

89. Regarding the projected emigration of wagoner
    Joh[ann] Herr of Flörsbach to (4)   New England, 1767
                                               [in fact, Pennsylvania]

90. Details regarding certain families from the
    district offices [Ämtern] of Bieber and Lohr-
    haupten who emigrated between August 1765 and
    13 February 1767, and the consequences thereof
    (4)   --, 1767

Following is an index of all the names appearing in the pre-
ceding translation, with annotations whenever they could be identified in the ship entry lists and oaths of allegiance for the port of
Philadelphia, as shown in Strassburger's and Hinke's *Pennsylvania
German Pioneers* (abbreviated S&H hereinafter). Particularly important
in the identification is the comparison of emigration dates as shown
in the Hanau manuscript with those shown in the Philadelphia ship
entry lists. Even more positive identification can be made in the
numerous cases where several family heads, listed together in the
Hanau manuscript, also appear together in the Philadelphia records.
And, since oaths of allegiance were required of all males over 16
years of age at Philadelphia, we frequently learn the probable iden-
tities of boys listed only as unnamed accompanying family members in
the Hanau document. The number which follows each name in the following index refers to the entry number in the translation.

Anweiler, Michel, 57

Arnold, Lorentz, 64; arrived
at Philadelphia 23 Oct 1754 on
Snow Good Intent from Amster-
dam via Gosport; note also
William Arnold not shown in
Hanau list, S&H 1:656-659

Aschermann, Johann Henrich, 65;
listed as John Henry Ashman
in American lists; arrived
at Philadelphia 21 Oct 1754
on *Bannister* from Amsterdam
via Cowes, S&H 1:646-7

Aumüller, Conrad, 64; listed as
Conrad Omiller in American

lists; arrived at Philadelphia
on 23 Oct 1754 on *Snow Good Intent* from Amsterdam via Gosport;
apparently accompanied by a
Johannes Aumiller, not listed in
Hanau list, S&H 1:656-658

Bar, Ulrich, 6

Bauer, Johann, 86; arrived at
Philadelphia 26 Oct 1767 on
Britannia from Rotterdam via
Portsmouth, S&H 1:717

Bausum, Johann, 45; this may be
the Johannes Bausum who arrived
at Philadelphia 21 Jul? 1751,
on *Two Brothers* from Rotterdam

via Cowes. Note also Philippus Bausum not listed in Hanau manuscript, S&H 1:465

Bautz, Johann Philip, 1

Bechtold, Friedrich, 26

Bechtoldt, August, 4

Beck, Peter, 49

Bender, Johann Georg, 8

Bender, Johann Philip, 71; a person of this name immigrated to Philadelphia 21 Oct 1754 on *Friendship* from Amsterdam via Gosport. This may have been the person who returned to Hanau a decade later. If so, researchers will wish to consider the possibility that others of this surname immigrating with him in 1754 (S&H 1:642, 644) were sons, and thus not listed in the Hanau manuscript

Bock, Johann, 64; this is probably Johannes Buck on lists; arrived at Philadelphia 23 Oct 1754 on *Snow Good Intent* from Amsterdam via Gosport; qualified same date but not listed as having taken oath of allegiance, S&H 1:656-7

Bolaender, Jacob, 61, 64; listed as Hannes or Johannes Bolander in American lists; arrived at Philadelphia 23 Oct 1754 on *Snow*

Good Intent from Amsterdam via Gosport; note also Johann Adam Bohlender on list B only; S&H 1:655, 657-8

Bopp, Mathaeus, 58

Bopp, Niclas, 68

Bopp, Valentin, 68

Brettmann, Wilhelm, 78

Brodt, Peter, 28

Bruder, Conrad, 63

Burghard, Sylvester, 35

Christ, Nicolaus, 30; arrived at Philadelphia 7 Sep 1748 on *Hampshire* from Rotterdam via Falmouth, S&H 1:373-375

Cloos, Thomas, 31; this might be Thomas Klosse who arrived at Philadelphia 13 Aug 1750 from Rotterdam via Portsmouth, S&H 1:430

Cress. *See* Kress

Deckmann, Johann Henrich, 51

Dietrich, Johann Adam, 87; listed as Adam Ditterich in American lists; arrived at Philadelphia 23 Nov 1767 on *Britannia* from Rotterdam via Portsmouth, S&H 1:717

Dietrich, Johann Henrich, 78

Dietz, Jonas, 33; listed as Johannes Tiets in American list A and Jonas Dietz in lists B

and C; arrived at Philadelphia
25 Oct 1748 on *Patience and Mary*
from Rotterdam via Leith, Scot-
land; note also Johann Michel
Dietz not listed in Hanau manuscript, S&H 1:386-389

Döll, Erasmus, 70

Döll, Henrich, 46

Döll, Melchior, 29

Dörr, Johann, 11, 28

Doll, Philip, 59; probably the J.
Joha[nn] Fill[ip] Diel who
accompanied Kleinfeller; arrived at Philadelphia 14 Sep
1751 on *Duke of Bedford* from
Rotterdam via Portsmouth, S&H
1:459

Eckel, Johann Henrich, 38; probably Henrich Eckel who arrived
at Philadelphia 26 Sep 1749 on
Ranier from Rotterdam via England, S&H 1:412

Emmerich, August, 23

Emrich, Johann Henrich, 72

Emrich, Johann Jacob, 80

Engel, Caspar, 49

Engel, George, 49

Euler, Christian, 15

Euler, Jacob, 15

Euler, Urban, 18

Faulstroh, Conrad, 63

Fischer, Conrad, 27

Fischer, Michel, 46; this might
be the immigrant who arrived
at Philadelphia 27 Sep 1752 on
President from Rotterdam via
England, S&H 1:490

Fischer, Reinhard Friedrich, 64;
listed as Friedrich Reinhard
Fischer in American lists;
arrived at Philadelphia on 23
Oct 1754 on *Snow Good Intent*
from Amsterdam via Gosport,
S&H 1:656, 657, 659

Flach, Johann, 79; this might
be Johann Adam Flick who arrived with Johann Henrich Ulrich at Philadelphia 23 Sep
1766 on *Chance* from Rotterdam
via Cowes, S&H 1:709

Förter, Adam, 28

Frantz, Hans George, 52

Frischkorn, Johann Georg, 37

Gieseman, Clemens, 1; related to
the Johan George Wilhelm
Geeseman/Güssemann who arrived
at Philadelphia 26 Oct 1741 on
The Snow Molly from Rotterdam
accompanying Stephan Rüb, S&H
1:313-315

Gilzinger, J. G., 64

Guthmann, Johann, 10

Hadermann, Christoph, 10

Haeuser, Conrad, 64; listed as

Conrad Heisser/Heysser in American lists; arrived at Philadelphia 23 Oct 1754 on *Snow Good Intent* from Amsterdam via Gosport; note also Johannes (Hannes) Heisser not listed in Hanau manuscript, S&H 1:656-659

Haffner, Michel, 10

Hansel, Adam, 20

Hansel, Michel, 20

Hartig, Johann Caspar, 23

Hartmann, Peter, 47; arrived at Philadelphia 12 Sep 1750 on *Priscilla* from Rotterdam via Cowes, S&H 1:444

Hartmann, Valentin, 85

Haydt, Nicolaus, 51

Heck, Philip, 20

Hedderick, Johann Peter, 8

Henning, Johann Martin, 37

Henss, Johann, 87; shown as Johannes Hem; arrived at Philadelphia 23 Nov 1767 on *Britannia* from Rotterdam via Portsmouth, S&H 1:717

Herr, Johann, 89; arrived at Philadelphia 9 Nov 1767 on *Minerva* from Rotterdam via Cowes, S&H 1:718

Herr, Peter, 54; could be the immigrant who arrived at Philadelphia 14 Sep 1751 on *Duke of Bedford* from Rotterdam via Portsmouth, S&H 1:459

Hess, Johann, widow of, 72

Hess, Johann George, 72

Heyer, Johann Wendel, 8

Heyer, Wilhelm, 78

Heyliger, Johann, 37

Hildebrand, Conrad, 37

Höck, Friedrich, 36; probably the Johann Friedrich Höck who arrived at Philadelphia 26 Sep 1749 on *Ranier* from Rotterdam and England; note also Johann Conrad Hock, not listed in Hanau manuscript, S&H 1:412

Hora, Johann Valentin, 68

Horch, Johann, 78

Huffnagel, Johann, 52, 62; listed as Johannes Hufnagel; arrived at Philadelphia 4 Oct 1752 on *Neptune* from Rotterdam via Cowes, S&H 1:493

Huth, Daniel, 60; although no person of this name is listed in S&H, an interested researcher might wish to consider the possibility that he was a family head who may have died before arrival in America. There are two immigrants, Valentin Huth and Michael Huth arriving at Philadelphia 14 Sep 1751 on *Duke of Bedford* from Rotterdam via Portsmouth, upon which a number of other Hanau subjects immigrated to America; the two immigrants, if accompanying sons of Daniel, would not have been listed in the Hanau manuscript, S&H 1:458

Huth, Johann, 47; arrived at Philadelphia 12 Sep 1750 on *Priscilla* from Rotterdam and Cowes, S&H 1:444

Ickus, Johann Friedrich, 74-1/2

Ickus, Martin, 64

Iffland, Georg, widow of, 11

Jost, Conrad, 28

Justheimer, Johann, 63

Kalbhen, Johann Philip, 19

Kautz, Christian, 62; arrived at Philadelphia 4 Oct 1752 on *Neptune* from Rotterdam via Cowes; note also Johannes Kauz, not listed in Hanau manuscript, S&H 1:494

Kaysser, Velten, 41; although there is no person of this name on extant ship arrival lists, attention is called to Ekhart and Leonhart Keyser who arrived at Philadelphia 26 Sep 1749 on *Ranier* from Rotterdam and England, S&H 1:411. It may be that Velten, the father, died before arrival and his sons, not listed in the Hanau manuscript, survived him; this hypothesis

is suggested because the two Keysers appear on the same ship list with Reinhard Rohrbach, with whom they may have come to America

Kester, Henrich, 5

Kiesling, Johan Christoph, 62

Kleinfeller, Johann Peter, 59; listed as Hans Petter Kleinfelter in American lists; arrived at Philadelphia 14 Sep 1751 on *Duke of Bedford* from Rotterdam via Portsmouth; note also Gerg and Johannes Kleinfelter, not listed in Hanau manuscript, S&H 1:459

Kleiss, Anna, 57

Kling, Anna Margarete, 43

Knöpp, Mathaeus, 24; this is probably Mathias Knip, age 48, who was sick upon arrival at Philadelphia 7 Oct 1748 on *Hampshire*, S&H 1:373

Köhler, Peter, 25

Köller, Johann Adam, 53

König, Johann Henrich, 33

Koller, Peter, 14

Kollip's widow, 52

Kollmann, Johann, 20

Koppel, Conrad, 69

Krafft, Johann George, 72

Kreckel, Adam, 32

Kress, Johann Peter, 62; although Johann Peter Kress and Niclas

Kress are not listed in S&H, researchers should consider immigrants, Johann, Henry, Caspar,
and Carls Kress, who arrived at
Philadelphia 4 Oct 1752 on *Neptune* from Rotterdam via Cowes.
It might be that J. Peter and
Niclas Kress, who were heads of
family in Hanau, died before
arrival, and the above four
were accompanying sons who
would not have been listed in
the Hanau manuscript; there
were a number of Hanau emigrants aboard this ship, S&H
1:493

Kress, Niclas, 62; see note on
Johann Peter Kress above

Kückendörffer, Frantz, 22

Kunckel, Eberhard, 25; this person is not identifiable in
ship lists containing other
names in this Hanau group

Kunckel, George, 48; shown as
George Cunkel on American
lists; arrived at Philadelphia
12 Sep 1750 on *Priscilla* from
Rotterdam via Cowes, S&H 1:444

Kunckel, Johann, 21

Lauch, Caspar, 6

Lauffer, Johann Henrich, 70

Lehning, Philip, 38; probably the
Johann Philip Lehmig who arrived

at Philadelphia 26 Sep 1749
on *Ranier* from Rotterdam via
England, S&H 1:412

Leiss, Johann Philip, 8

Lentz, Anna Catharina, 29

Lind, Anna Elisabeth, 50

Lohra, Conrad, 64; listed as
Conrad Lorey in American lists;
arrived at Philadelphia 23 Oct
1754 on *Snow Good Intent* from
Amsterdam via Gosport; see
also Johann Caspar Lohra and
Johannes Lohra (Lorey), not
listed in Hanau manuscript,
S&H 1:656-658

Lotz, Johann, 20

Lotz, Johann Wilhelm, 37

Lotz, Wilhelm, 62; listed as
Johann Wilhelm Lotz in American lists; arrived at Philadelphia 4 Oct 1752 on *Neptune*
from Rotterdam via Cowes; see
also Nicolas Lotz not listed
in Hanau manuscript, S&H 1:494

Lubke, George, 62a

Manckel, Johann Philip, 69

Matern, Christian, 4

May, Johann, 1

May, Johann Conrad, 69

Meffert, Aegidius, 34; arrived
at Philadelphia 15 Sep 1748
on *Two Brothers* from Rotterdam
via Portsmouth; see also Johann

Schmidt, Thomas, 8

Schmitt, Theobald, 39

Schraid, Philip, 63; shown as
Philip Schreid and Johann Philip
Schreidt in American lists; ar-
rived at Philadelphia 21 Oct 1754
on *Friendship* from Amsterdam via
Gosport, S&H 1:642, 644

Schroeder, Henrich, 20

Schuhermann, Ludwig, 10

Schum, Christoph, 58

Schussler, Johann Henrich, 7

Schuster, Johann Peter, 87

Schuster, Melchior, widow of, 87;
although this woman is not shown
on American lists, attention is
called to Peter Schuster, shown
in the ship lists but not in
Hanau manuscript, who might have
been a son; arrived at Philadelphia 23 Nov 1767 on *Britannia*
from Rotterdam via Portsmouth,
S&H 1:717

Schwind, Peter, 84

Seiffart, Johann, 11

Seybold, Johann, 66; shown as Johannes Seyboldt in American
lists; arrived at Philadelphia
21 Oct 1754 on *Friendship* from
Amsterdam via Gosport; note also
Philip Seibolt who does not appear in Hanau manuscript, S&H
1:644

Specht, Conrad, 3

Staaf, Johann Henrich, 88

Steffel, Johann Valentin, 16

Steigerwald, Friedrich, 87;
arrived at Philadelphia
26 Oct 1767 on *Britannia*
from Rotterdam via Ports-
mouth, S&H 1:717

Steigerwald, Georg, 25; shown
as Yerick Styerwald in American list A, George Steyer-
wald in list B, Georg Steyer-
wald in list C; arrived at
Philadelphia 7 Sep 1748 on
Hampshire from Rotterdam via
England, S&H 1:373-376

Steigerwald, Johann, 86; arrived at Philadelphia 26 Oct
1767 on *Britannia* via Cowes,
S&H 1:717

Stock, Lorentz, 13

Stock, Michel, 58

Stock, Nicolas, 75

Strohl, Peter, 31; shown as
Peter Strall in American list
A, Peter Strohl in lists B & C;
arrived at Philadelphia 25 Oct
1748 on *Patience and Margaret*
from Rotterdam via Leith, Scot-
land, S&H 1:387-389

Strohlipp, --, widow of, 44

Topfer, Balthasar, 9

Traut, Andreas, 69

Ulrich, Johann Henrich, 79; arrived at Philadelphia 23 Sep 1766 on *Chance* from Rotterdam via Cowes, S&H 1:709

Urich, Michel, 30; shown as Michael Orig in American list A, Johan Michel Ohrig in lists B and C; arrived at Philadelphia on *Hampshire* 7 Sep 1748 from Rotterdam via Falmouth, S&H 1:373-376

Velten, Johann, 72

Völcker, Johann Georg, 17

Waitz's widow, 63

Weber, Johann, 9, 15

Wegmann, Paul, 11

Wehrheim, Conrad, 63

Wentzel, Johann Henrich, 4

Wentzel, Lorentz, 30; arrived at Philadelphia 7 Sep 1748 on *Hampshire* from Rotterdam via Falmouth, S&H 1:373-376

Wentzel, Philip, 30

Wetzel, Nicolaus, 37

Weymar, Caspar, 55; shown as Caspar Weimmer in American lists; arrived at Philadelphia 14 Sep 1751 on *Duke of Bedford* from Rotterdam via Cowes, S&H 1:458

Wiessner, Conrad, 40; probably the Conrad Wysner who arrived at Philadelphia 24 Aug 1749 on *Elliot* from Rotterdam via Cowes, S&H 1:390

Winckelmann, Johann, widow of, 67

Wirth, Peter, 11

Zeth, Johann Martin, 12

FOOTNOTES

1. Marburg. Staatsarchiv. Bestand 80. Hanau Geheimer Rat. Band II. The section of interest is Rubrik XXXII, beginning at page 1025.

2. Ralph Beaver Strassburger and William J. Hinke, *Pennsylvania German Pioneers: A Publication of the Original Lists of Arrivals in the Port of Philadelphia from 1707-1808.* 3v. Philadelphia, 1934. Reprint ed. v. 1, 3 only; Baltimore: Genealogical Publishing Co., 1966. [Filby No. 3020].

3. *See* Clifford Neal Smith and Anna Smith *geborene* Piszczan-Czaja, *Encyclopedia of German-American Genealogical Research* (New York: R. R. Bowker Co., 1976), 109, 126.

4. Despite the fact that some emigrants named herein were probably non-conformists to the prevailing Evangelical Lutheran state church, researchers finding names of interest to them should apply to the Evangelische Pfarramt in the village of origin for vital data, because many sectarians were christened or married in the state church, since the ceremonies of non-conforming congregations or groups were strictly controlled, often suppressed, by the governments of most principalities.

5. The fact that the register summarizes a package of papers leads to the suspicion that a further search of the holdings of the Staatsarchiv Marburg might uncover useful subsidiary documentation, particularly inventories of taxable possessions, and the actual emigration petitions.